THE JEWISH AMERICANS

Designed by Philip Clucas
Edited by David Gibbon
Commissioning Editor: Andrew Preston
Photographic Research: Leora Kahn and
Meredith Greenfield

MALLARD PRESS
An imprint of BDD Promotional Book Company, Inc.,
666 Fifth Avenue, New York, NY 10103
Mallard Press and its accompanying design and logo
are trademarks of BDD Promotional Book Company, Inc.
CLB 2734
© 1992 Colour Library Books Ltd., Godalming, Surrey, England.
First published in the United States of America
in 1992 by The Mallard Press
Printed and bound in Hong Kong
All rights reserved
ISBN 0 7924 5562 2

THE JEWISH AMERICANS

J. J. Goldberg

MALLARD PRESS

CONTENTS

AMERICA'S PROMISE OF freedom has been a powerful symbol to Jews throughout her history. Left: Jewish children, rescued from Nazi-ruled Vienna in June 1939, arrive in New York where they will be adopted by American families. Previous page: Jews celebrate outside the Washington office of the Zionist movement as Israel declares independence, May 14, 1948.

Introduction

OR MORE THAN A century, ships pulling into New York Harbor have been greeted by the monumental Lady Liberty, her torch borne 300 feet above the water as a beacon. At her feet is a plaque inscribed with a poem, *The New Colossus*, written in 1883 by the Jewish-American poetess Emma Lazarus:

"Keep, ancient lands, your storied pomp!" cries she,
With silent lips. "Give me your tired, your poor,
Your huddled masses yearning to breathe free,
The wretched refuse of your teeming shore,
Send these, the homeless, tempest-tost to me.
I lift my lamp beside the golden door!"

Like most American Jews then and since, Emma Lazarus grew up more American than Jewish, knowing little of her religious heritage. During a chance visit

RIGHT: POLISH JEWS, fleeing the devastation of World War I, wait in Danzig for passage to America. Left: Russian-Jewish immigrants pass the Statue of Liberty, from an 1892 engraving. Above: Emma Lazarus (1849-1887), the Jewish poetess whose "The New Colossus" is affixed to the statue's base.

to the harbor, she came across a throng of Russian-Jewish refugees fleeing czarist persecution. The rest of her too-short life was devoted to helping impoverished Jewish immigrants, as expressed in her famous poem. Lazarus died in 1887; her poem was affixed to the statue's base in 1903.

Thus it was that a Jew's greeting to her co-religionists came to constitute America's best-known message to the world. Despite the nation's overwhelming Christian majority, this is oddly appropriate. For of all the "tempest-tost" refugees who have come in search of America's promise, no group has had more reason to be grateful than the Jews. No land has ever given them safer haven.

Strange to tell, though, the birth of the American Jewish community was pure accident. The first 23 Jews were dumped on the docks of Manhattan in September 1654 by an unfriendly sea captain who refused to carry them further.

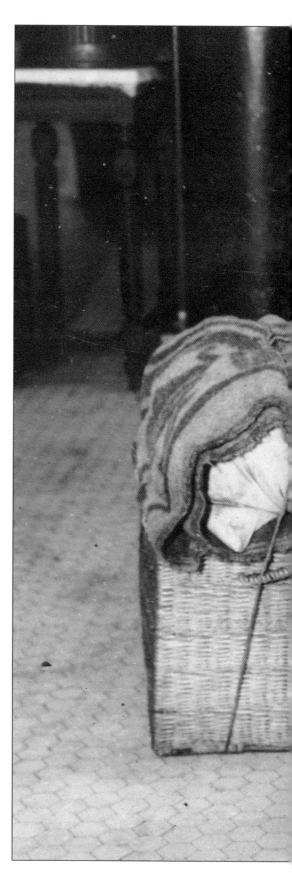

ABOVE: LADY LIBERTY holds her torch aloft, overlooking New York Harbor as it appeared in the placid 1950s. Right: immigrant children in 1910 wait with their baggage in the entrance hall at Ellis Island, America's main immigrant entry station.

AMERICA LED THE FREE WORLD *against Nazism, but her own gates had been closed to refugees in 1920 by rising isolationism. Below: passengers on the S.S.* St. Louis *in Antwerp, Belgium, in June 1939 at the end of her "Voyage of the Damned." She carried 1,128 German Jews who sailed the Atlantic in a vain search for safe harbor. Twenty-two were admitted to Cuba, 288 to Great Britain. The rest returned to the continent, most to death at Nazi hands. Right: two German Jews find U.S. haven, December 31, 1938. Left: Albert Einstein (1879-1955), the renowned German-Jewish physicist, celebrates his 70th birthday at home in New Jersey with a group of European children who survived the Holocaust. With him is William Rosenwald, chairman of the United Jewish Appeal.*

CHAPTER ONE

Before America

THE STORY OF AMERICAN JEWS properly begins in the ancient birthplace of the Jews, biblical Judea. Conquered by Roman legions, the Jews rose up between 70 and 135 A.D. in a series of failed revolts. In the ensuing repression hundreds of thousands were exiled to Europe, Africa, even India. In each new home they settled in close-knit communities, governed by the strict rules of their religion.

As Europe became Christian, Jewish communities were placed under harsh restrictions. They were forced into enclosed areas, barred from most occupations, cruelly taxed and periodically set upon by mobs. All Jews were expelled from Germany in 1182, from England in 1290, from France in 1394 and from Austria in 1421.

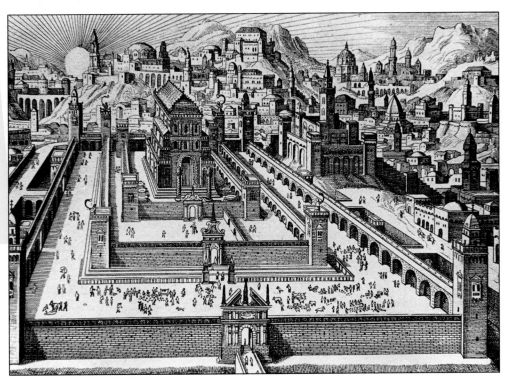

RIGHT: SOLOMON'S TEMPLE in ancient Jerusalem, from a 1650 engraving. Above: a high priest of the modern-day Samaritan sect observing Passover on Mt. Gerizim. Left: the Star of David, carved into the wall of Jerusalem.

P. B: Bouttats fec. Aqua Forti

CHRISTOPHER COLUMBUS'S VOYAGE from Spain, launched two days after the expulsion of Spanish Jewry, stumbled on a New World and transformed Jewish history. Right: Columbus (1451-1506) hears his men cry out, "Land!," from an undated woodcut. Left: Columbus's third landfall, at Haiti, November 1492. Many scholars believe Columbus may have been a converted Jew. Certainly his key backers and some crew were secret Jews. His translator, Luis de Torres, baptized a Christian just days before the voyage, was the first European to settle in America.

ABOVE: RABBI ISAAC ABOAB DE FONSECA (1605-1693), the first rabbi in the New World, settled in Dutch Recife in 1642. When the colony fell to the Portuguese in 1654 he fled back to Amsterdam.

Islam was kinder than Christendom. Especially in Moslem Spain, Jewish life blossomed in a 500-year Golden Age coinciding with Europe's Dark Ages. But the Christian reconquest ended the Spanish Jews' freedom. Many were forced into baptism; suspected backsliders – "Marranos," or secret Jews – were tortured by the Inquisition. Finally, in March 1492, Queen Isabella ordered the expulsion of all Spain's half-million Jews. Thousands, in panic, adopted Christianity. At least 300,000 fled; some to distant Turkey or Holland, most across the border to Portugal. In 1497 Portugal forced all its Jews to convert.

Two days after Isabella's expulsion deadline, on August 3, 1492, the Genoan sea-captain Christopher Columbus sailed west from Spain in search of a new trade route to India. He found instead a new world. Tens of thousands of Spanish and Portuguese colonists flocked there over the next century, among them thousands of Marranos seeking a place to continue their secret worship.

In 1630, the Portuguese Brazilian colony of Recife was captured by the Protestant Dutch, and the Marranos threw off their masks. Joined by colleagues from all over South America, they built a thriving Jewish community. In 1654, Portugal recaptured Recife. All 5,000 Jews were forced to flee for their lives.

One group of 23 Recifeans, beset by storms and pirates, was picked up by the French trading ship *St. Charles*. Her captain decided to drop his unwanted passengers at his next Dutch port of call. This happened to be a rude outpost, Fort Nieuw Amsterdam on Manhattan Island, in untamed North America.

Nieuw Amsterdam's irascible Governor Peter Stuyvesant had so far kept his backwater post free of dissenters, and he ordered the 23 Jews to leave. They appealed to their brethren in Amsterdam, some of whom owned stock in the Dutch West India Company, Stuyvesant's employer. The board of directors ruled the Jews could stay.

Stuyvesant conceded, on condition that the newcomers care for their own poor, refrain from erecting a house of worship, and pay a head-tax in lieu of militia duty. Within months, two of the settlers, Jacob Barsimson and Asser Levy, protested the tax and won the right to stand guard. The building of a synagogue waited until Nieuw Amsterdam was taken by Great Britain in 1664 and renamed New York. The third condition – caring for their own – has been honored to this day.

Above: ships of the Dutch West India Company, operator of Dutch colonies in the Americas. Right: Peter Stuyvesant, the governor of Nieuw Amsterdam, surrenders his colony to the British in 1664.

CHAPTER TWO

The Colonial Era and the Young Republic

OR A CENTURY NORTH America attracted few Jews, although a tiny group of Dutch Jews arrived in 1658 in Newport, Rhode Island, and a few dozen Spanish Jews came to Georgia in late 1733. The first synagogue, New York's Shearith Israel ("the Remnant of Israel"), was erected only in 1728.

By the time of the Revolution in 1776, the Jews' numbers had grown to about 2,500, a small fraction of the colonies' four million total. The majority made their living as petty merchants, although a few, like Moses Lindo of Charleston and Aaron Lopez of Newport, achieved renown in shipping and international trade.

The Revolution found American colonists divided bitterly into pro- and anti-British factions. Not so the Jews; with few exceptions, they favored independence, and some paid dearly for it. Francis Salvador, a captain in the South Carolina militia, became in July 1776 the first Jew to fall in America's defense. Haym Salomon of Philadelphia, deputy treasurer of the United States, bankrupted himself paying the republic's bills and died a pauper.

America was demonstratively grateful to her Jewish citizens. President George Washington, visiting Newport in 1790, greeted the Jewish congregation there with a letter that sums up America's promise:

"The Citizens of the United States of America have a right to applaud themselves for having given to mankind examples of an enlarged and liberal policy," he wrote. " … For happily the Government of the United States, which gives to bigotry no sanction, to persecution no assistance, requires only that they who live under its protection should demean themselves as good citizens in giving it on all occasions their effectual support."

Washington wrote two similar letters, one to the Jewish congregations of Savannah, and the other to the congregations of New York, Philadelphia, Richmond and Charleston. Those four had banded together in 1789 in the first abortive union

LEFT: HAYM SALOMON (1740-1785), a trader in charge of brokering America's Revolutionary War bonds. Above: Isaac De Lyon, a leader of the early Jewish community in Savannah.

THE FIRST JEWS IN *North America had no rabbis to lead them, and were dependent on older Jewish communities in Amsterdam or the Dutch Caribbean. Left: Rev. Gershom Mendes Seixas (1745-1816), lay minister of New York's Congregation Shearith Israel. He was one of the invited clergy at the inauguration of President George Washington in 1789. Right: the synagogue in Charleston, South Carolina, built in 1795 but burnt down in 1838. The painting is dedicated to the congregation's minister, Rev. Gustavus Poznansky, by the Jewish artist Solomon Nunez Carvalho.*

ABOVE: MATSAH, the flat bread eaten by Jews during the eight-day Passover festival, was baked in every community where Jews lived.

of American Jews. Newport and Savannah stayed aloof, disliking the union's leader.

It was the first of many times American Jewry tried and failed to form an all-inclusive confessional union. America's absolute freedom of conscience, denying religion any legal power over the individual, has proved both a blessing and a curse in Jewish community-building.

The First Amendment to the U.S. Constitution ordered Congress to "make no law respecting an establishment of religion, or prohibiting the free exercise thereof." The 13 states were a different story; most chose to limit the right of voting and public office to Christians. A few, like New York and South Carolina, adopted full equality from the outset. Others continued legal barriers as late as 1876. Still, America was freer than any country Jews had ever known, and such limits seemed petty.

LEFT: MORDECAI MANUEL NOAH (1785-1851), U.S. consul in Tripoli, sheriff of New York, judge, journalist and playwright. A fiery defender of Jewish rights, he tried to build a Jewish homeland on an island in Niagara Falls, but no one settled there.

ABOVE: REBECCA GRATZ (1781-1869), pioneer Philadelphia philanthropist. A legendary beauty, she was Sir Walter Scott's model for the character Rebecca in Ivanhoe. *Never married, she devoted her life to service, founding America's Jewish immigrant aid society, the first Hebrew Sunday school and a non-sectarian children's relief fund. Right: the "Jew Bill," introduced into the Maryland state legislature every year from 1816 until it finally passed in 1825. It gave Jews the right to hold office in that state, which had been founded as a haven of religious tolerance – for Catholics. The last states to lower religious restrictions were North Carolina in 1868 and New Hampshire in 1876.*

If America gave Jews a rare freedom to practice their religion, it also made them free not to. Many were doubtless scrupulous in the rules of Sabbath and kosher food, but most were not. There were no rabbis to guide them, only a few lay ministers who could lead prayers, officiate at weddings and teach the children simple lessons. When complex questions of ritual law required a rabbi's ruling, letters were sent to the rabbis in established communities in Curaçao or Amsterdam. More often, no questions were asked.

Perhaps the best measure of their piety is the fate of their descendants: out of all the famed Jewish clans of colonial America – Seixas, Nones, Gomez, Lopez, Hart – only a few scattered offspring are still Jewish. The rest faded into Christian America long ago.

PROCEEDINGS IN THE

Legislature of Maryland,

DECEMBER SESSION, 1818,

ON WHAT IS COMMONLY CALLED

The Jew Bill;

CONTAINING

THE REPORT OF THE COMMITTEE

APPOINTED BY THE HOUSE OF DELEGATES

"To consider the justice and expediency of extending to those persons professing the Jewish Religion, the same privileges that are enjoyed by Christians:"

TOGETHER WITH

The Bill reported by the Committee,

AND

THE SPEECHES

OF

THOMAS KENNEDY, Esq. OF WASHINGTON COUNTY,

AND

H. M. BRACKENRIDGE, Esq. OF BALTIMORE CITY.

Baltimore:
PRINTED BY JOSEPH ROBINSON,
Circulating Library, corner of Market and Belvidere-streets.

1819.

CHAPTER THREE

The Coming of the Germans

HE END OF THE Napoleonic wars in 1815 sparked a wave of repression throughout Central Europe, touching off a mass flight to America. Thousands of Jews were among the emigrants, increasing the U.S. Jewish population to 50,000 souls by 1848. In that year, a wave of failed revolutions in the German states sent another two million refugees across the Atlantic, many of them Jews. By 1860, the community was approaching 200,000.

The German Jews introduced to America the beginnings of a classic Jewish community. They brought the first ordained rabbis to North America. They established an ethnic press and formed the first national Jewish fraternal order, B'nai B'rith, in 1843. When anti-Jewish outrages occurred in Damascus in 1840, American

WITH THE MASS MIGRATION of German Jews in the first half of the 19th century, American Jewry grew from an exotic footnote into a stable, thriving community. Jews spread from a few coastal cities into the interior of the American continent, as far as the Pacific. Left: Julius Meyer (1851-1905), a German-born merchant, settled in Nebraska where he became an Indian trader, interpreter and trusted adviser to the Plains Indian chiefs. Right: frontier Jews on community picnic in Helena, Montana. Seated second from left, in white hat, is the community's leader, Rabbi Samuel Schulman.

Jews held mass meetings to demand U.S. intervention; the first time, but not the last, that American Jewry mobilized in behalf of Jews elsewhere.

Before the Germans came, America had boasted six synagogues, all following the Sephardic rite of Spanish-Portuguese Jews. Now dozens of Ashkenazic or German synagogues sprang up alongside them. German Jews spread to new cities along the Atlantic coast, into the interior and as far west as San Francisco.

Most Germans arrived penniless. Thousands sought a livelihood as peddlers, loading up packs of cloth and notions and heading into the wilderness. A few parlayed their trades into legendary fortunes: Nathan and Isidor Straus, born in

Above: a rabbi supervises the kneading of dough for matsah, from the 19th-century Frank Leslie's Popular Monthly.

Bavaria, who turned the R.H. Macy Company into America's first great retailing chain; Levi Strauss, the Bavarian-born tailor whose reinforced blue jeans made his descendants one of the leading families of San Francisco; Adolph Ochs, born in Cincinnati of German parents, who turned the New York Times into one of the world's great newspapers.

One of the German Jews' most profound contributions – some question its benefits – was the European-Jewish custom of sectarian quarreling. Many of the newcomers adhered to the fledgling German movement for Jewish Reform. They prayed in the vernacular rather than in Hebrew, left their heads uncovered and brought organs into the synagogue, violating an ancient rabbinic ban on instrumental

THE GERMAN JEWS *quickly entered mainstream America, some rising to heights of wealth and success, others helping to build a strong foundation for Jewish community life. Left: Levi Strauss (1831-1902), Bavarian-born dry-goods peddler who joined the Gold Rush in 1849. His denim "blue jeans" were popular among the miners. Right: Rabbi Isaac Mayer Wise (1819-1900), one of the young rabbis who came to America in the German immigrant wave. He became the leader of Reform Judaism.*

ABOVE: ADOLPH OCHS *(1858-1935), son of a German-born U.S. Army officer, pictured in 1896 as he took over the ailing* New York Times.

THE STRUGGLE BETWEEN TRADITION and Reform divided American Jews throughout the 19th century. Left: Reform leader Isaac Mayer Wise, pictured with the sculptor Moses Ezekiel, tried to create an all-inclusive Union of American Hebrew Congregations in 1873, but the traditionalists quickly walked out. Above left: Wise's great opponent, Rabbi Isaac Leeser (1806-1868), who came to Philadelphia from Germany in 1824. A preacher, publisher and biblical translator, he was the first national spokesman for tradition; his disciples founded Conservative Judaism.

THE DEBATE OVER SLAVERY found most American Jews united in favor of abolition, though a few defended slavery on biblical grounds. Left: August Bondi (1833-1907) came to America from Austria after the failure of the 1848 revolution there. He settled in Kansas, where he joined John Brown's anti-slavery guerrillas. Right: Rabbi David Einhorn (1809-1879), Hungarian-born leader of Reform Judaism's radical wing. He settled in Baltimore in 1855, but in 1861 fled for his life amid mob protests at his fiery abolitionist sermons.

music in prayer. By 1840, feuds over Reform were splitting congregations all across America.

The religious debate brought two German-born rabbis to national fame. One, Isaac Leeser of Philadelphia, was an eloquent defender of tradition. The other, Isaac Mayer Wise of Cincinnati, was a fiery Reformer. Wise hoped to unify American Jews, and when he convened the first conference of America rabbis in 1855, even Leeser attended. But Wise's Reform views alienated the traditionalists, and when he finally created his Union of American Hebrew Congregations in 1873, it was firmly Reform.

By 1885, radical Reformers had disavowed Talmudic law and the restoration of Zion. They even served forbidden shrimp at a formal dinner. The very next year, Leeser's successors laid the foundations for a separate movement, eventually known as Conservative Judaism.

As JEWS FOUND ACCEPTANCE, their religious festivals sometimes became high-society events. Above: the annual Purim costume ball at New York's Academy of Music, March 14, 1865, from a contemporary engraving.

At the height of the German Jews' mass flight to freedom, America itself was torn apart by a debate over freedom for enslaved black Americans. The slavery question was rapidly plunging the nation toward Civil War.

Blacks were the worst victims of American bigotry, but they were not the only ones. Since 1845, the Native American or "Know-Nothing" Party had agitated for an end to Catholic and Jewish immigration. Jews found their best defense was to ally themselves with advocates of equal rights for all. In the slavery debate, most Jews favored abolition.

When Civil War came in 1861, most Jews were loyal to the states in which they lived. Four-fifths lived in the North, but thousands of Jews fought in both armies, from drummer-boys to generals. Two Jewish members of the U.S. Senate, David

WHEN THE CIVIL WAR came, most Jews sided with the states where they lived. Left: the colorful Judah P. Benjamin (1811-1884), "the brains of the Confederacy." A brilliant orator, he was elected to the U.S. Senate from Louisiana in 1858, but left Washington in 1861 to join the Confederacy. Named attorney general, he rose to secretary of war and finally secretary of state. After the collapse of the South in 1865 he fled to England, where he enjoyed a second career as a distinguished barrister. Above: Confederate currency, with Benjamin's portrait in the upper left-hand corner.

JEWS WERE NUMBERED both among the heroes of Southern patriotism and those who profited from human slavery. Bottom: Captain E.J. Levy of the Richmond Light Infantry Blues. Right: an advertisement for a Georgia slave-trader.

NEGROES, NEGROES.

The undersigned has just arrived in Lumpkin from Virginia, with a likely lot of negroes, about 40 in number, embracing every shade and variety. He has seamstresses, chamber maids, field hands, and doubts not that he is able to fill the bill of any who may want to buy. He has sold over two hundred negroes in this section, mostly in this county, and flatters himself that he has so far given satisfaction to his purchasers. Being a regular trader to this market he has nothing to gain by misrepresentation, and will, therefore, warrant every negro sold to come up to the bill, squarely and completely. Give him a call at his Mart.

J. F. MOSES.

Lumpkin, Ga., Nov. 14th, 1859.

Jews served with distinction in the U.S. military, but equality came only with struggle.
Left: Commodore Uriah P. Levy (1792-1862), one of America's most decorated military figures, whose fiery defense of Judaism embroiled him in duels and court-martials. He single-handedly ended flogging in the U.S. Navy, and at his bequest the ancestral home of Thomas Jefferson was made a permanent monument to American democracy.
Right: Brigadier General Edward Salomon (1836-1913), one of five Jewish generals serving the North in the Civil War. He commanded a heavily-Jewish Illinois regiment. After the war he served as governor of Washington Territory in the Pacific Northwest, and later was elected to the California state legislature.

Above: Ulysses S. Grant, commander of the Union armies and 18th president of the United States. His "Order No. 11" of December 1862, intended to enforce a trade embargo on the South, singled out "Jews as a class." It was the gravest single act of government anti-Semitism in U.S. history.

Yulee of Florida and Judah P. Benjamin of Louisiana, left Washington to join the Confederacy. Benjamin served as its attorney-general, secretary of war and finally secretary of state.

In the heat of the Civil War, America had her first taste of the ancient evil of anti-Semitism. Especially in the South, groaning under a Northern blockade, Jewish shopkeepers were often blamed for the hardships. Jews were attacked in speeches, rallies, even local ordinances. Journalists delighted in blaming the South's woes on "Judas Iscariot Benjamin."

The most serious attack – indeed, the gravest anti-Jewish government act in American history – was the Northern army's "Order No. 11" of December 17, 1862. Issued by General Ulysses S. Grant, the order expelled from occupied Tennessee "the Jews, as a class violating every regulation of trade established by the Treasury Department." Its purpose was to stop illegal cross-border trade with the enemy, but it caused such an outcry that President Lincoln cancelled it two weeks later.

CHAPTER FOUR

The Jews of Russia and the Great Immigration

MERICA'S BLOODY STRUGGLE ECHOED throughout the world. In Germany and Italy, the triumph of American federalism helped spur new struggles for national unity. In feudal Russia, the image of freedom inspired Czar Alexander II to experiment with reforms, such as freeing the serfs. He also moved to ease the lot of the world's largest and most miserable Jewish community.

The five million Jews of Russia were a huge accident, inherited when the czars annexed bits of their native Poland in 1772 and 1796. For centuries before they had lived uneasily along the 1,000-mile arc of the medieval Polish empire, stretching from the Baltic to the Black Sea. Untouched by modern culture, governed by their own rabbis, speaking their own language called Yiddish, they poured their energies into talmudic learning. The czars welcomed them into Russia with draconian restrictions on residence, work and movement.

In the early 19th century, breezes of Western modernity began touching Russian Jews; with Alexander II's Lincoln-inspired reforms of 1862, a "Jewish Enlightenment" exploded in a flowering of Yiddish art and literature. But the flowering was short-lived. In April 1881 a fanatic assassinated Czar Alexander II. His son, Alexander III, blamed the Jews and sent his secret police to incite murderous mob attacks on Jews across Russia. Within a month new laws were imposed, harsher than ever. The government's open goal was to eliminate Russian Jewry by forced conversion, forced emigration or death.

Russian Jewry responded with three great answers that have shaped all Jewish life since then: Zionism, socialism, and America.

America in 1881 was in its Gilded Age. The railroad had united the two coasts and the central plains were being cleared for a breadbasket. Oil and electricity were transforming industry. As the saying had it, the business of America was Business. Between 1880 and 1920, into that yawning labor market poured some 23 million

LEFT: THE GREAT HALL at Ellis Island in New York Harbor, the immigrants' gateway to America for a half-century. Above: Jacob Schiff (1847-1920), German-born philanthropist, and co-founder of the American Jewish Committee.

Two MILLION JEWISH IMMIGRANTS poured into the United States between 1881 and 1924 from the desperate poverty of Russia, Romania and Austro-Hungary. Most settled first in the teeming ghetto of New York's Lower East Side. Today most American Jews are two generations removed from the poverty of the ghetto, but the experience still colors Jewish cultural and political attitudes. Left: housewives buy vegetables on Hester Street, 1914. Above: a suspender salesman hawks his wares, c. 1900.

immigrants from the backwardness of southern and eastern Europe. Over two million were Russian Jews.

Most Russians came first to the Lower East Side of Manhattan, a dense ghetto of crowded tenements. There they recreated their Yiddish-speaking society, with its rabbinic academies and revolutionary cells, Yiddish theaters and newspapers and vegetarian societies.

The German Jews greeted the newcomers with mixed feelings. After a half-century in America they had won economic success and some social acceptance. Though largely excluded from polite society, they had created their own social world of clubs, private schools and charities. As the Russians flooded America's cities with their strange dress, habits and smells, the Germans felt their hard-won respectability threatened.

WHILE THE RUSSIAN JEWS' mass immigration to the Lower East Side captured popular imagination, other groups of Jews were also coming in – and some had other destinations in mind, outside New York. Above: Syrians on New York's Lower West Side at the turn of the century. About 40,000 Syrian Jews came to America, eventually settling in Brooklyn where they remained largely isolated from the larger Russian community until the 1970s. Right: a Russian Jew who went west, Isaac Bender, aboard his peddler's wagon in rural Ohio in 1919.

THE POVERTY in the swelling
Russian-Jewish ghettos sparked an
outpouring of idealism among
better-established German Jews.
Below: Lillian Wald (1867-1940),
a pioneer in American social work
and founder of the Henry Street
Settlement on the Lower East Side.
Left: Wald in 1919 with British
Labour politician Ramsay
MacDonald and his daughter.

THE EXPLOSIVE GROWTH of the
American Jewish community
touched off a building boom,
sometimes jokingly referred to as
U.S. Jewry's "Edifice Complex."
Grand Jewish structures became
commonplace even in remote
corners of the American frontier.
Top right: Yeshiva University of
New York, founded as a rabbinical
seminary in 1886, today a major
university and a world center of
Orthodox Judaism. Far right: the
Jewish Theological Seminary of
America, founded in New York in
1886. Right: Temple Emanu-El of
Helena, Montana, one of some
4,000 synagogues in America.

Yet they rose to the occasion. In New York and elsewhere they organized charitable societies to care for the penniless newcomers. They built hospitals and clinics, orphanages, old-age homes and youth centers for the tenement dwellers. Some, like the legendary Lillian Wald and Henrietta Szold, actually moved into the slums and devoted their lives to working with the poor.

No mere charity could meet the needs of the Great Immigration, however. By 1905 a million Russian Jews had come, mostly to New York. At the time the city's entire population was only about four million.

THE LOWER EAST SIDE spawned a self-contained Jewish society with Jewish shops and customers, Jewish bosses and workers, Jewish newspapers decrying Jewish injustices. The Yiddish daily Forward *wrote during a 1901 strike: "It is a domestic matter. The workers are ours and the bosses are ours…" Below: a Jewish family spends its evening together, doing low-wage garment "piece work" c. 1900. Left: a Lower East Side street scene, c. 1910.*

Vast numbers of the immigrants worked in ready-made garment manufacturing, a stepchild of the Industrial Revolution. It was a world of small businesses that employed a few dozen workers each in small, unventilated lofts. Most often, employer and employees alike were Jewish. That did not prevent horrific conditions from arising, giving birth to a new word: "sweatshop."

Public debate in the ghetto was dominated by radical ideas brought from Russia. When the Socialist Party U.S.A. was formed in 1897, it first publication was a Yiddish daily newspaper, the *Forward*, which grew to become one of America's most influential metropolitan dailies and spawned a dozen imitators. For many years the lone Socialist in the U.S. Congress was Meyer London of the Lower East Side.

Far more popular than socialist parties, however, were trade unions that promised higher wages instead of theory. The founding president of the American Federation of Labor (AFL), Samuel Gompers, was a Yiddish-speaking, Jewish cigar-maker from London. Gompers championed a distinctly American breed of apolitical "business unionism." Asked once what the workers wanted, Gompers replied: "More."

Most of the Russian-Jewish garment workers found Gompers' unionism too tame. A more radical style marked the "Jewish needle-trade unions," the International Ladies Garment Workers Union and the Amalgamated Clothing Workers, leading to bitter strikes in the decade before World War I. The disputes between Jewish bosses and their workers became so disruptive of New York City life that the organized Jewish community stepped in to mediate.

THE POVERTY ON THE LOWER EAST SIDE sparked national outrage. Muckraking journalist Jacob Riis, in his 1890 book How the Other Half Lives, *wrote: "…the children of the poor grow up in joyless homes to lives of wearisome toil that claims them at a young age when the play of their happier fellows has just begun." Right: a sweatshop in the 1880s, photographed by Riis. Above: workers in Moe Levy's garment shop, 1912.*

THE FORMATION OF the Garment Unions on the eve of World War I gave a voice to the Jewish immigrant workers but sparked feuds between socialists and anarchists, revolutionaries and reformers, Yiddishists and assimilationists. Right: union leaders count ballots in a 1915 strike vote. Below: workers rally at Union Square, New York, before the bitter Cloakworkers' strike of 1913.

EVEN MORE DIVISIVE were the efforts to organize the furriers, whose violent 1912 strike was settled only after the intervention of the "Uptown" liberal Rabbi Judah Magnes, head of the New York Kehillah. Left: angry demonstrators during a 1926 furriers' strike wave copies of the communist Yiddish newspaper Freiheit.

In this way the pains of the Great Immigration planted the seeds of a truly organized Jewish community, something that had eluded American Jewry for two centuries. Its first goals were to remove from the public eye the most embarrassing by-products of the immigration: labor war and ghetto crime.

Some sociologists believe organized crime springs up naturally in immigrant communities, as a crude mediator between confused newcomers and their new home. In America , the Jewish ghettos spawned what many non-Jews saw as a veritable "Hebrew crime wave." Pastors and editors railed against it. One legal scholar, Frank Moss, wrote: " … the criminal instincts that are so often found naturally in the Russian and Polish Jews … warrant the opinion that these people are the worst element in the entire make-up of New York City."

In 1908 the New York City police commissioner, Theodore Bingham, proposed special ethnic detective squads to infiltrate the gangs. Today this is standard police strategy, but then it sparked a furious outcry from the Jewish community. Bingham was forced to back down.

The Jewish community responded to Bingham in 1909 by forming the New York Kehillah (Hebrew for "community"), a federation of some 200 organizations that for a brief decade united Russians and Germans, Reform and Orthodox, socialist and capitalist in one governing body. It mediated major garment strikes, imposed some order on the gang-ridden Lower East Side and even supervised kosher food.

RIGHT: ABE "KID TWIST" RELES, a top "Murder Inc." hitman, arrested in 1940. He offered lengthy confessions, terminated when he fell to his death from a Brooklyn hotel window. Far right: Arthur "Dutch Schultz" Flegenheimer, legendary Bronx bootlegger. His pathological violence alarmed other mob leaders and he was murdered in 1935, on orders from "Lepke." Below far right: Louis "Lepke" Buchalter, founder of "Murder Inc.," after his surrender to J. Edgar Hoover in 1939. An underworld kingpin and master labor-racketeer, he was convicted of murder and executed in 1944. Below right: Herman Rosenthal, one of New York's earliest Jewish mobsters.

THE JEWISH GANGSTER ERA began on the Lower East Side at the turn of the century and ended with the death of Meyer Lansky (right) in 1983. Above: Nathan "Kid Dropper" Kaplan, leader of an early Jewish gang on the Lower East Side, murdered by a rival gang in 1923. Jewish gangs faded away after World War II, when most leaders were jailed or killed. A few continued into the 1950s and '60s, but their children did not follow them into crime. Today's American Jews are noted for their abhorrence of violent crime.

April in Paris
book to the
Peaks Library

WELCOME

860-
55 0,0641

WE PROTEST AGAINST.
THE CONTINUED SLAUGHTER
OF INNOCENT JEWISH
MEN, WOMEN AND CHILDREN
IN POLAND.

CHAPTER FIVE

The Community Finds a Voice

ORE ENDURING THAN THE Kehillah was the American Jewish Committee, created in 1906 by a group of 50 leading German-Jewish businessmen and lawyers. It arose in response to a new wave of anti-Jewish repression that swept Russia following the failed revolution of 1905. The committee's founders hoped to influence the U.S. government to act on their co-religionists' behalf. But some Russians suspected a crasser motive: improving Jewish life under the czars so as to stem the tidal wave of immigration.

Despite its detractors, the Committee quickly came to be the acknowledged voice of American Jewry. It established cordial ties with two other national bodies, B'nai B'rith and the Union of American Hebrew Congregations. It worked for the rights of others, including pioneer efforts on behalf of black Americans. As anti-Semitic outrages in Russia grew in intensity, the Committee helped move the U.S. government to speak out. Shortly after the Committee's formation, President Theodore Roosevelt appointed its best-known leader, Oscar Straus, as his secretary of commerce, the first Jew to serve in a U.S. cabinet. "I want," Roosevelt wrote, "to show Russia and some other countries what we think of the Jews in this country."

Most Russians spurned the Committee, however. The Yiddish press called it undemocratic, elitist and worse. Far more popular among the poor "downtown" Jews were those groups that arose on the eve of World War I to demand the most decisive emancipation possible: restoration of the Jews to their ancient homeland in the land of Zion.

World War I was devastating to East European Jewry, which lived in the path of some of the fiercest fighting. American Jews organized to provide relief to the war zone, but they were divided along ethnic and political lines. In 1916 the three main groups merged into the Joint Distribution Committee, the first large-scale effort of a united American Jewry. "The Joint" still oversees Jewish welfare efforts from Romania to Ethiopia.

AMERICAN JEWS WERE galvanized to action by their brethren's suffering in Europe. Left: Jews rally in 1919 for the rights of Polish Jewry, shattered by World War I. Above: Theodore Roosevelt, the first president to name a Jew to his Cabinet. As New York police commissioner in 1895, Roosevelt permitted a visiting German anti-Semite to address a crowd, but assigned him an all-Jewish police escort.

As the new century opened, Jewish life was beginning to flourish. Seminaries were training native-born rabbis, and a new, American school of centrist Judaism, called Conservatism, was evolving. Above: Solomon Schechter (1850-1915), longtime president of the Jewish Theological Seminary. Left: the Central Conference of American Rabbis convenes in 1897 at Atlantic City. Rabbi Isaac Mayer Wise is seated at center.

The formation of "the Joint" prompted calls for Jewish unity to be expanded beyond the charitable sphere into the political. There were efforts to form a united American Jewish delegation to the peace conference that was to convene after the war's end. The conference was to carve up Europe's aging empires into their long-suppressed ethnic components, freeing nationalities like those of Lithuania, Hungary and Bulgaria. Jewish goals at the Paris Peace Conference were twofold: winning guarantees of civil rights for Jews in the new Europe, and gaining recognition for the Zionist nation-building project in Palestine.

THE RHYTHMS OF American Jewish life centered on family gatherings, holiday celebrations and mutual aid. Top left: a cooking class for girls, and (above) a painting class for boys, in community-run trade schools for poor Jewish youths. Left: a Jewish family gathers c. 1908 in the sukkah, the hut traditionally erected each autumn to mark the week-long Feast of Tabernacles. Right: "When a Jew eats a chicken one of them is sick" [folk-saying about Jewish poverty]: preparing the Sabbath chicken on the Lower East Side, 1928.

Zionist and socialist groups sought to ensure that American Jewry would be represented not by a brokered delegation of the rich, but by an elected American Jewish Congress. The negotiations dragged on for years. Opposition was led by leaders of the American Jewish Committee, who feared open balloting might elect a slate of revolutionaries. At length nationwide elections were held in 1917. The Congress convened that December, and was disbanded after the Paris Peace Conference of 1922.

Historians still speak of the American Jewish Congress as a high point in the community's history. Few others know of its existence. It was revived a decade later, but now it was just one more Jewish organization.

CHAPTER SIX

The Jazz Age

T HE 1917 AMERICAN JEWISH Congress elections drew 133,000 voters, but more than a million American Jews did not vote. To many immigrants and their children, America was a place to escape the confines of their past.

The 1920s were a wide-open time. It was "the Jazz Age," an era of short skirts and long weekends. Like each wave of Jewish immigrants before them, the Russians and their children were attracted by the openness of American life. Many had scraped together enough money to escape the tenements and move to better neighborhoods. Judaism increasingly became a matter of nostalgia and family reunions.

AMERICA WAS WIDE open in the Jazz Age, and young Jews often found themselves torn between two worlds. Left: Al Jolson in the landmark film The Jazz Singer. *Above and right: a Boston Jewish family, the Millers, enjoying the good life in the '20s and '30s.*

THE OLD WORLD OF AMERICAN JEWRY *was close-knit, often with several generations living under the same roof. Father and sons frequently went into business together, and hard work usually brought a measure of prosperity. Above: three generations gathered around the holy day candles, from a New Year's greeting card. Right: the Greenfeld family of New York City, c. 1900.*

DECEMBER · 1910 ·

Records for the Edison Phonograph

SOPHIE TUCKER, an Exclusive Edi

THE NEW WORLD *of limitless opportunity was epitomized by the entertainment industry. Young Jews streamed into popular music at the turn of the century, into Hollywood films after World War I, into television after World War II. Above: popular songwriter George Gershwin (1898-1937) achieved a rare respect in the classical world with crossover works like "Rhapsody in Blue" and "Porgy and Bess." Above right: Sophie Tucker (Kalish) (1884-1966) had a giant hit in 1925 with "My Yiddishe Mama."*

JEWS AND NON-JEWS mingled in Hollywood with a gaiety that masked the film industry's hard-driving business atmosphere. The industry was largely founded by a small group of Jewish entrepreneurs, and their work helped define the American self-image in this century. Right: Jack Warner (1892-1978), youngest of the four Warner (originally Eichelbaum) Brothers, flanked by actress Marlene Dietrich and actor Errol Flynn. Below: Louis B. Mayer (1885-1957), founder of Metro-Goldwyn-Mayer studios.

LEFT: FILMMAKER David O. Selznick, L.B. Mayer's son-in-law, watches (at left) as actress Vivien Leigh signs on to play the role of Scarlett O'Hara in his 1939 MGM production, Gone With the Wind. *Already signed and looking on are Leslie Howard and Olivia De Haviland.*

Jews did not just join the Jazz Age; they helped to create it. It was a time when new inventions – the phonograph, the motion-picture camera, the radio and the microphone – were transforming leisure pursuits into the world's first "entertainment industry."

The explosion of Jewish talent in the communications media during the first half of the century was so extraordinary that scholars are still struggling to grasp it. Some ascribe it to inbred talent, nurtured through centuries of ghetto life. Others note that Jews traditionally enter new fields of economic endeavor whenever they are excluded from old ones. A few extremists have even tried to label it a "Jewish conspiracy."

What is certain is that from the end of the 19th century Jews formed a huge percentage of songwriters, vaudeville performers and impresarios. After World War I, so many Russian immigrants flocked to California to create the motion-picture industry – especially the founders of the great movie studios: Sam Goldwyn and Louis B. Mayer of M-G-M, Harry Cohn of Columbia and the Brothers Harry, Sam and Jack Warner of Warner Brothers – that one acclaimed history of the industry was titled, *How the Jews Invented Hollywood.* A generation later, television was transformed from a toy into an empire by the Russian-Jewish entrepreneurs who built the three networks: William Paley at CBS, David Sarnoff at NBC and Leonard Goldenson at ABC.

A SEPARATE WORLD of Yiddish-language theater and film flourished between 1880 and World War II. It produced some leading stars, like Paul Muni and Edward G. Robinson, and won critical acclaim. But its audience dried up as younger Jews abandoned Yiddish for English, and the reserve of Yiddish-speaking immigrants was ended by the Nazis. Left: a 1931 movie poster for the first Yiddish musical talkie. Right: the Artef Players, an avant-garde New York Yiddish repertory company, perform The Outlaw in 1936.

ABOVE: THE IRREPRESSIBLE GAMINE of the Yiddish theater, Molly Picon (1898-), featured in one of her 1920s hit plays on Second Avenue, the Lower East Side's "Yiddish Broadway."

Almost as extraordinary as the Jews' embrace of the media was their near-total invisibility in the art they created. This was largely due to their belief that mainstream America was not interest in seeing them. Tolerant as America might seem, it was still a Christian country. Acceptance, many believed, depended on Jewish assimilation. Most of the best-known Jewish entertainers changed their names: Israel Baline to Irving Berlin, Asa Yoelson to Al Jolson, Fanny Borach to Fanny Brice, Emanuel Goldenberg to Edward G. Robinson.

Just as striking was the avoidance of Jewish themes outside the cloistered Yiddish theater. Other groups' legacies were sentimentalized in popular songs like *Ireland Must Be Heaven* and *Marie From Sunny Italy*, but Jewish topics were a rarity. Irving Berlin, America's most beloved and prolific songwriter, scored his biggest hit in 1945 with *White Christmas*, the best-selling pop song of all time. Yet he never wrote a significant Jewish song.

To some extent, the invisibility of the Jewish past was due to the Jews' own ambivalence. Many had only bad memories of "the Old Country," with its cruel laws, its anti-Semitic violence and its interfering rabbis.

Nowhere were these misgivings depicted more graphically than in *The Jazz Singer*, Hollywood's first talking picture. In it Al Jolson played a Jewish youth who runs off to become an entertainer rather than follow his stern father as cantor in the synagogue. The landmark film, one of the early Hollywood's very rare Jewish images, seems almost autobiographical in depicting the film makers' view of Judaism.

There was good reason for a Jew to seek invisibility in the 1920s. Beneath the gaiety of the Jazz Age lurked a darker tide of rising nativism and race hatred. The first great feature-length film produced in America, D.W. Griffiths' 1915 *The Birth of a Nation*, was a paean to the anti-black, anti-Catholic, anti-Jewish Ku Klux Klan.

TELEVISION, LIKE FILM, was transformed into a major industry by a small group of Jewish entrepreneurs. Below: William Paley (1901-1991), founder of CBS, launches the first radio network broadcast.

THE FIRST TALKING PICTURE, The Jazz Singer, was the story of a cantor's son who runs off to become a popular entertainer. Al Jolson (1886-1950) saw it as a reprise of his own life and he insisted on the role. The 1927 film revolutionized the movies. Above: Jolson as the Jazz Singer, with Warner Oland and Eugenie Besserer as his parents. Right: two giants of the musical stage, composer Jerome Kern (1885-1945) and librettist Oscar Hammerstein II (1895-1960), work on their classic Show Boat. Opposite: "Mr. Television," Milton Berle (1908-) (Mendel Berlinger), hams it up with guest Ethel Merman (Ethel Zimmerman) on his "Texaco Star Theater."

A DARK TIDE of nativist reaction arose on the eve of World War I with the revival of the anti-black, anti-Jewish Ku Klux Klan. After the Russian Revolution in 1917 the U.S. government joined the right-wing panic and thousands of radicals were imprisoned or deported, including many immigrant Jews. Right: Leo Frank, a Jewish business-man lynched by a Christian mob in Georgia in 1915. Left: anarchist firebrand Emma Goldman (1869-1940) addresses a Union Square crowd in 1916. She was deported to her native Russia in 1919.

Two years before *The Birth of a Nation*, a Jewish factory manager named Leo Frank was convicted of murdering a Christian child in Georgia. The trial was conducted in such an ugly atmosphere of anti-Semitic mob threats that the governor of Georgia finally pardoned Frank in 1915 and ordered him freed. Instead, he was kidnapped and lynched. Frank's martyrdom sparked national outrage.

Prejudice and xenophobia seemed to sweep America during and after World War I in waves of hysteria, first against anything German, then against "Reds." Both fell heavily on Jews. Thousands of trade unionists and radicals were arrested; some were even deported to Russia. Around the nation, a revived Ku Klux Klan attracted some four million members.

Even auto magnate Henry Ford joined the hate campaign; in 1920 he launched a national magazine called *The Dearborn Independent*, which spewed monthly venom about "the International Jew, the world's foremost enemy." Ford recanted publicly in 1927, but his essays are still reprinted today by extremist groups.

Most Americans shunned the nativist tide, but it had one devastating effect: Congress was moved to enact sharp restrictions on immigration in 1920 and again in 1924. The goal was to reduce the influx of "bolsheviks" from Eastern and Southern Europe. The result would be to trap million of Jews in Nazi-ruled Europe.

AMERICAN JEWRY'S GERMAN elite reacted to the dislocations of the 1920s with calm determination. Above: banker-diplomat Henry Morgenthau, Sr. (1865-1940) and New York Times publisher Adolph Ochs, en route to the 1929 convention of the Union of American Hebrew Congregations in San Francisco.

EXPERIENCE

Among the Ku-Klux.

HARTFORD:
PUBLISHED BY THE AUTHOR.
1872.

CHAPTER SEVEN

Mr. Roosevelt and Mr. Hitler

B Y 1930 THE AMERICAN Jewish population had reached nearly five million, almost four percent of the nation. Most had now left the ghettos and moved their families to greener, suburban vistas. Even with the economy mired in the Great Depression, Jews felt America was good to them. Anti-Semitism for most was a distant echo or an occasional annoyance. European fascism had its American sympathizers in the '30s, but they had little influence. Both political parties clung firmly to American traditions of fair play.

The Democratic Party in particular took up the cause of trade unions, immigrants and minorities and forged them all into a majority coalition behind Franklin D. Roosevelt's social-democratic "New Deal." Jews were prominent in

As THE NAZI CLOUD gathered over Europe, America seemed to offer hope. Left: Franklin D. Roosevelt is greeted by crowds in Atlanta, Georgia, during his 1932 campaign for the presidency. Above: Adolf Hitler, chancellor of Nazi Germany. Right: Albert Einstein, the world-renowned physicist, is sworn in as a U.S. citizen in 1940.

THE SPECTER OF NAZI PERSECUTION spurred renewed Jewish efforts on behalf of the Zionist homeland in Palestine. American Jews built homes, schools and factories in the Holy Land while seeking diplomatic support for Jewish statehood. This page: American Zionist leader Henrietta Szold (1860-1945), on a 1934 visit to Palestine, is greeted by German-Jewish children rescued from Europe through her efforts.

PRESIDENT FRANKLIN ROOSEVELT had many Jewish advisers, and he fought hard to bring America into the war against Nazism. When the war came he bent every resource toward victory; historians would later accuse him of ignoring the mass murder of European Jews. Above right: Rabbi Stephen S. Wise (1874-1949), leader of the American Jewish Congress and a White House intimate, defended Roosevelt in public. Above: Louis D. Brandeis (1856-1941), the leader of American Zionism and the first Jew to serve on the U.S. Supreme Court. Though a liberal, he opposed Roosevelt's radical domestic programs.

Roosevelt's inner circle, including his Treasury secretary, German-Jewish aristocrat Henry Morgenthau Jr., and the charismatic head of the American Jewish Congress, Rabbi Stephen S. Wise. More than the leaders, though, average Jews across America took "FDR" to their hearts. His picture graced the walls of many Jewish homes and he won over 90 percent of Jewish votes. More than any other modern figure, he cemented the century-old idea that Jewish security in America was best ensured by guaranteeing security for all.

There was, of course, a great shadow lying across the heart of the mid-20th century; the horror of Nazism. For 12 years between 1933 and 1945, Adolf Hitler and his minions ravaged Europe, racing to complete their mad schemes of genocide. From 1941 to 1945 six million Jews – two of every five Jews in the world – were systematically murdered by the German killing machines.

The Jews of Europe did not merely face mass killing; they faced utter annihilation, with no hope of appeal or escape, while the rest of the world looked on. Nothing like it has ever been conceived by civilized human beings, before or since. Many Jews today find it incomprehensible that the community did not rise up in anger and force Roosevelt to take action. For example, they complain, the Allies could have bombed the concentration camps to stop the killing.

The Jews of America did take to the streets during the 1930s. They demonstrated, urged boycotts of German goods, demanded diplomatic efforts to save European Jews. In 1938 they organized the United Jewish Appeal, combining immigrant aid, Zionist efforts and international relief work into a single, powerful fund-raising campaign. When the war in Europe began, Jews rallied to prod America into the fight.

In hindsight, historians agree that they might have done more. But American Jewry in 1942 had no sense of itself as a power broker. They were five million, outnumbered by 130 million non-Jews who did not feel involved. American Jews themselves felt vulnerable.

ACROSS AMERICA JEWS marched, rallied and fasted during the 1930s and 1940s to end Nazism, but it was not enough. Below: a march through downtown Chicago in May 1933 draws an estimated 25,000 Jews demanding an end to Nazism. Right: a group of Orthodox rabbis marches on Congress, accompanied by commanders of the Jewish War Veterans, demanding U.S. military action to save European Jewry from the Nazi death camps,

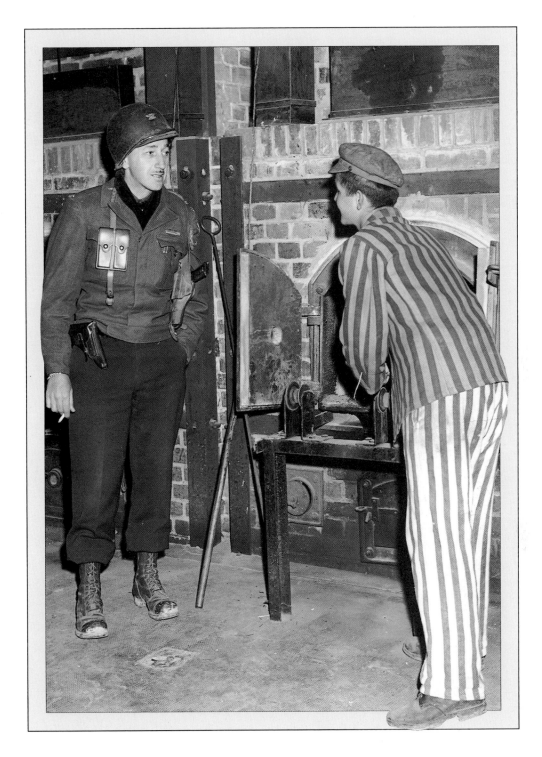

DESPITE THE PLEAS of her Jewish citizens – 550,000 of whom joined the U.S. Army to fight Hitler – America admitted fewer than 175,000 European Jews during the Nazis' long reign. It was only at the war's end, when Allied troops entered the death camps, that the world realized the full horror of the Holocaust. Left: a group of 50 Viennese-Jewish children, brought to America for adoption, enters New York Harbor in June 1939. Above: an inmate at the Dachau concentration camp shows the crematoria to Colonel Walter O'Brien of the U.S. 7th Army, April 30, 1945.

LEFT: PRAYERS OF THANKS at the war's end. A group of Austrian-Jewish refugees, interned during the war as aliens at a camp in northern New York, offers prayers after learning that President Truman has given them permission to remain in America.

NEW YORK BECAME the battleground in the fight for Jewish statehood when the United Nations took up the issue after 1945. American Jews mobilized to win international recognition of the Jewish nation. Above: Rabbi Abba Hillel Silver (1893-1963), leader of the American Zionist movement, argues before the U.N. in November 1947.

With the fall of Nazi Germany in 1945, the full extent of the Holocaust became clear. Beyond the unspeakable human suffering, the Nazis had utterly destroyed world Jewry's heartland in Eastern Europe. American Jewry, a stepchild of Jewish history only a decade earlier, suddenly found itself to be the largest and most powerful Jewish community in the world.

Two great tasks now faced this community. One was to rehabilitate the shattered remnant of European Jewry. The other was to ensure that such destruction never recurred by at last giving the Jews a homeland of their own. Between 1945 and 1948 virtually every Jewish institution in America was bent to the twin tasks. Even non-Zionist groups like the American Jewish Committee and the Reform movement joined the battle, which ended with the establishment of the State of Israel in 1948.

Some had feared the establishment of Israel might cast doubts on the loyalty of American Jews, but instead it gave them new security. Most seemed to feel for the first time as though they had a homeland to look back to with pride, like the Irish, the Italians and other "hyphenated-Americans." Many liked to quote the late Justice Brandeis, who had said that to demand a homeland for the Jews was the ultimate expression of democracy and Americanism.

It was in many ways the beginning of a Golden Age for American Jewry. And with growing security came a lessened need for invisibility. Now, as Jews moved into the American mainstream, they took Judaism with them. They constructed

FIVE ARAB NATIONS went to war in 1948 to block the formation of the U.N.-mandated Jewish state. American Jews raised funds, worked to secure U.S. recognition of Israel, and as the war dragged on, secretly acquired arms and materiel for the embattled state. Right: Israeli soldiers capture the Arab town of Ramleh, June 1948. Bottom right: members of the Haganah survey the ruins of a captured Palestinian town. Below: Chaim Weizmann, Israel's first president, presents President Truman with a Torah scroll in thanks for U.S. recognition of the young Jewish state.

gleaming synagogue buildings in their new neighborhoods, rivaling their neighbors' churches for grandeur. They built Hebrew schools, community centers, rabbinical academies and distinguished universities, including the renowned Brandeis University and the Orthodox-sponsored Yeshiva University.

Not all Jews saw America's openness as an invitation to join the broader culture. Some, including thousands who came from Europe after World War II, wanted only the chance to preserve their old culture undisturbed. These Orthodox

LEFT: ISRAEL'S FIRST anniversary, in May 1949, draws over 150,000 Jews to New York's Madison Square Park. Below: Bess Myerson. the first Jewish Miss America, in 1945. Below right: Orthodox Jews in traditional garb.

Jews adhered to the strict rules of rabbinic law, rejecting even the hesitant modernisms of Isaac Leeser's Conservative disciples. They lived in their own neighborhoods, created separate day-schools for their children, avoided social contact with non-Jews. Some refused to wear American-style clothes, preserving instead the black garb of medieval Poland.

But the vast majority of American Jews steered a middle course. They believed it was possible to join American society without abandoning Judaism. Several popular scholars tried in their works to capture the essence of this evolving, hybrid Jewish experience, especially Horace Kallen's theories of the American "melting-pot," and Will Herberg's *Protestant, Catholic, Jew.*

If the scholars were struggling to define the new hybrid, the Jews were simply living it with gusto. Each new Jewish conquest, whether large or small, became a cause for celebration: Louis D. Brandeis, in 1916 the first Jew on the Supreme Court; Charles Levine, in 1927 the first Jew to fly the Atlantic; "Hammering Hank" Greenberg, the fabled star of baseball's Detroit Tigers in the 1930s; and most of all, the beloved Bess Myerson, who in 1945 became the first Jewish "Miss America."

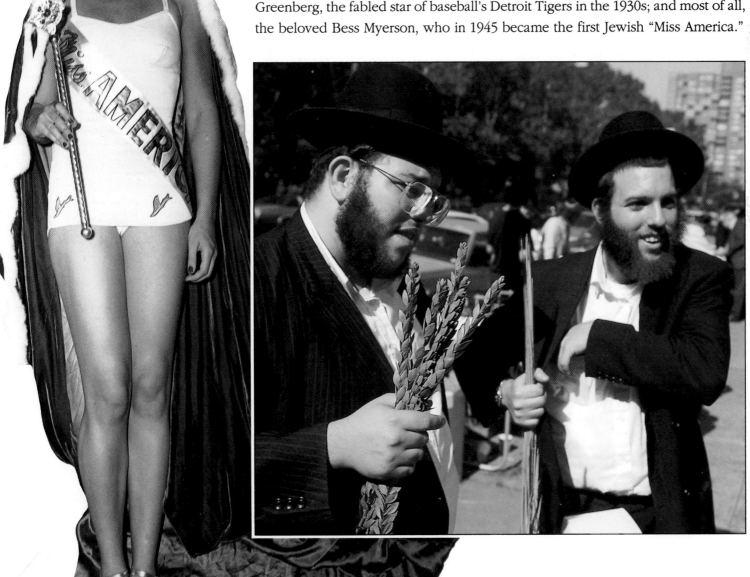

CHAPTER EIGHT

At Home at Last

More than ever, American Jews in the post-war era were convinced their safety lay in ensuring the welfare of all. Though firmly middle class, they remained overwhelmingly pro-labor and pro-Democrat, even as the rest of America moved rightward in the 1950s. They provided the strongest base of white support for black civil rights, donating heavily to the National Association for the Advancement of Colored People, and other black groups. Jewish lawyers like Jack Greenberg and Morris Abram won some of the blacks' most celebrated court victories.

Jewish political activism traditionally began with the premise that equal rights for all were the best safeguard of Jewish rights. Even after most Jews entered the middle class, they continued in the 1960s to work for labor and minority rights. The mood turned rightward in the 1970s, as community leaders focused on Israel and Soviet Jewry. Yet opinion polls showed Jews were still overwhelmingly liberal. Right: Rabbi Abraham Joshua Heschel (1907-1972), a revered theologian, joins with black leader Rev. Martin Luther King, Jr. in a 1965 "freedom march" in Alabama. Left: protesters rally in Washington in December 1987 to demand freedom for Soviet Jews. About 250,000 people marched in the rally, a high point in American Jewry's 20-year diplomatic campaign for Soviet-Jewish rights.

THE POSTWAR FIFTIES were a mixed time of rising achievement and political unease. Above: Albert Einstein celebrates his 72nd birthday at his Princeton home by presenting the "Albert Einstein Award" to physicist Julian Schwinger of Harvard University, just two decades after Harvard and Princeton had dropped their "Jewish quotas." Above right: Ethel and Julius Rosenberg are arraigned in 1951 on charges of passing atomic secrets to the Soviets. Left: filmmaker Louis B. Mayer testifies before the House Un-American Activities Committee, probing alleged communist infiltration in Hollywood. Above left: at decade's end, Jews in Boston protest the revival of the American Nazi Party.

As liberal as they were, few Jews still believed in socialism. An important minority, however, continued despite the Cold War to view communism as an idealistic crusade. The execution in 1953 of Julius and Ethel Rosenberg, Jewish communists convicted of spying for the Soviet Union, left widespread suspicion that anti-Semitism lurked in the background.

In the 1960s, several trends – the assassination of the youthful president John F. Kennedy, Southern white resistance to black rights, the unpopularity of the war in Vietnam – combined to foster a combustible atmosphere of radicalism among American youth. Nowhere was it stronger than among young Jews, raised from birth on liberalism. When the civil rights movement mounted interracial "freedom rides," flooding the South with activists, an estimated 40 percent of the white riders were Jews. Two of them, Andrew Goodman and Michael Schwermer, were killed by white racists and became martyrs in the civil rights cause. The protest songs of Bob Dylan, a young Jewish pop singer from Minnesota, came to symbolize the hopes of young America.

Postwar Hollywood no longer shrank from openly Jewish images, offering films like the 1947 Gentleman's Agreement, *about anti-Semitism, and the 1960* Exodus *about the birth of Israel. Above: "the Goldbergs," a 1950s television series about a Jewish family, starred Gertrude Berg as Molly and Philip Loeb as Jake. Above right: Barbra Streisand played Jewish vaudevillian Fanny Brice in the 1968 film* Funny Girl. *Right: Zero Mostel and Gene Wilder in* The Producers, *the 1968 black comedy about Jews and Nazis.*

Jewish intellectuals had a special place in American literature and thought in the postwar era. Right: Saul Bellow, author of the 1964 novel Herzog, *a landmark study of the alienation of the modern intellectual.*

Right: Erica Jong, whose blunt 1973 novel Fear of Flying *was a milestone in the sexual revolution. Above: Norman Podhoretz, editor of* Commentary, *a literary journal published by the American Jewish Committee, which became America's most influential intellectual forum in the 1970s and 1980s.*

In the turbulent sixties some Jews were leaders of the left-wing "youth rebellion," even as others continued their rise into "the Establishment." Left: Bob Dylan (Zimmerman), the eloquent rock-'n'-roll poet often described as "the voice of the Sixties Generation." Facing page: three Jewish justices of the U.S. Supreme Court – Arthur J. Goldberg (1908-90) (top left); Felix Frankfurter (1882-1965) (bottom left); and Abe Fortas (1910-82) (right). Frankfurter's succession to the seat vacated by Justice Brandeis in 1939 had confirmed what was known as "the Jewish seat" on the high court. When Frankfurter retired in 1962 the seat was inherited by Goldberg, a member of John F. Kennedy's Cabinet. Goldberg resigned in 1965 at the request of President Lyndon Johnson to become U.S. ambassador to the U.N., and Johnson appointed Fortas, an old friend. Fortas resigned amid political scandal in 1969 and no Jewish justices have been appointed since then. Coincidentally, all the Jewish justices before Fortas had distinguished records of Jewish community leadership. Fortas was the first Jewish justice married to a non-Jew, perhaps symbolizing the weakening loyalties of American Jews.

But in the mid-1960s some black leaders started calling for the expulsion of whites from their movement. The black demands were sometimes tinged with anti-Semitism, particularly as the Black Muslim movement gained strength. In 1968, black activists in New York demanded fewer white teachers in black neighborhoods; this threatened the jobs of thousands of Jews for whom the civil service had once been a ticket out of the ghetto. The black-Jewish confrontation in the New York schools gripped the nation's attention and proved to be a watershed in Jewish political attitudes. Over the next two decades black-Jewish tension rose and growing numbers of Jews lost faith in liberalism.

The conservative mood was reinforced by the Israel-Arab war of June 1967. The war was preceded by a month of noisy Arab saber rattling, mixed with non-stop threats to "drive the Jews into the sea." The days of waiting created an anxious sense among Jews around the world that a second Holocaust was looming. When war came, ending in a lightning Israeli victory and the reunification of Jerusalem, the terror gave way to near-messianic rejoicing.

But the Six-Day War left a bitter aftertaste. Many Jews now saw international opinion as callously indifferent to the fate of Israel, and by extension, of Jews everywhere. The sense of isolation grew apace during the 1970s as world sympathy shifted away from Israel toward Palestinian Arabs who vowed to destroy the Jewish state. In 1975, when the United Nations voted to condemn Zionism as a form of "racism," Jews throughout the world felt utterly betrayed and abandoned.

By the eighties, American Jews had become a proud, assertive community, influential in domestic affairs and respected around the world for their clout. Issues of concern to Jews, particularly Israeli security and Soviet-Jewish freedom, became important priorities on the national agenda. Left: Henry Kissinger, a 1939 refugee from Nazi Germany, became secretary of state in 1974 under President Richard Nixon. Responsible for the conduct of U.S. foreign policy around the globe, he would say in later years that he "never for a moment forgot" he lost most of his family in the Holocaust. Right: the New York Salute to Israel parade, an annual event drawing tens of thousands of observers, along with the nation's top politicians, proceeds up Fifth Avenue in May 1987. Below: a young demonstrator for Soviet Jewry.

Ironically, the rising sense of unease coincided with a period of unprecedented prosperity, influence and acceptance for American Jews. Statistics bore this out. Through some poverty remained, Jews had become America's most affluent and best-educated minority by 1980. Anti-Semitic attitudes had dropped to an all-time low. Yet Jewish fears of anti-Semitism rose to their highest level since World War II. The Holocaust, it seemed, loomed ever-larger in their memory as the years passed.

In politics, the endlessly-squabbling Jewish organizations had finally managed to forge an effective working structure that allowed them to speak with a single voice. Acting together, the community was able to exert enormous influence in Washington and nationwide. Much of its agenda — U.S. aid to Israel, freedom for Soviet Jews, remembrance of the Holocaust — was now standard U.S. policy. Virtually every door was open to Jews. Henry Kissinger, a Jewish refugee from Hitler's Germany, served as secretary of state, fifth in line to the presidency. In the U.S. Congress, Jewish representatives rose from a half-dozen in Franklin Roosevelt's time to a dozen in John Kennedy's, and nearly three dozen, eight percent of the total, in 1990.

Yet Jews dropped during that same period from four percent of the U.S. population to just over two percent. America had doubled in population in 50 years, but Jews had scarcely grown; affluence had led to a stagnant birthrate. In the 1970s a new wave of Jewish immigration poured into America from the Soviet Union, but its effects were offset by the numbers of Jews who married non-Jews and raised their children outside the community. By 1985, one of every two Jews was marrying outside the faith. A 1990 survey by the Council of Jewish Federations found a community with a Jewish "core population" of five-and-a-half-million, plus another two-million non-Jewish spouses and offspring of Jews. The leadership of the Jewish community faced the 21st century in a mood of crisis and foreboding.

EVEN AS JEWS ENTERED the heart of America, it could be said that America was entering the soul of Judaism. Below: Rabbi Sally Preisand, the first woman rabbi, was ordained at Hebrew Union College in 1973.

Despite the public fascination with Jews who intermarried and drifted away from tradition in the 1970s and '80s, a broad movement for Jewish cultural renewal was underway at the same time. Growing numbers of young people were training for the rabbinate, creating new forms of worship and reviving old ones. Jews combined religious, cultural and political activity to create a boisterous, diverse community life. Below: Rabbi Jack Bemporad, a Reform leader active in Jewish-Christian dialogue, coaches his son in blowing the ram's horn to usher in the New Year, 1966. Right: preparing for the New Year at an old-age home in New York, 1952.

Left: Jewish activists read from the Torah during a street-corner prayer service outside the Soviet mission to the United Nations, 1988.

Other studies pointed the opposite way, however, for those who were willing to look. Many children of mixed marriages continued to consider themselves Jewish, even when the mother was a non-Jew and the children were thus non-Jews by traditional rabbinic law. Even in the fourth and fifth generations after immigration, as many as 80 percent of all Jews continued to observe traditional Jewish holidays and give their children at least a minimal Jewish education. Growing numbers of non-Jewish spouses were serving in the Jewish community as volunteers, educators and synagogue leaders.

It seemed as the 21st century approached that America was producing a Jewish community in her own image: porous, irreverent, free-thinking, and blissfully ignorant of rabbinic lore. It was far from the sort of Jewish life nurtured by traditionalists down through the centuries. But American Jews were faithful in their own fashion, and they continued from one general to the next, defying the doom-sayers.

As AMERICA NEARED THE END of the 20th century, her Jewish citizens had become a vital part of her social fabric. Colorful, creative and outspoken, they left an indelible mark in a wide range of fields. Below far left: Woody Allen (Allen Koenigsberg) became America's most respected auteur filmmaker. Below left: Mel Brooks (Melvin Kaminsky) directed some of Hollywood's most off-beat movies in the 1980s. Far left: Ed Asner, crusty star of "Lou Grant" and other popular television shows, was a controversial union leader. Left: Henry Winkler won fame as the television character called "the Fonz," but won respect as a philanthropist and social activist. Above right: Edward I. Koch served 12 years as mayor of New York. His blunt style made him an international symbol of American-Jewish brashness. Below right: Bella Abzug served as a congresswoman from New York, but she won a permanent place as a symbol of outspoken feminism. Below: one Nobelist honors another as Elie Wiesel, the novelist and concentration camp survivor, presents his personal "Holocaust Remembrance Award" in 1991 to former Secretary of State Henry Kissinger. Looking on is Israeli diplomat Meir Rosenne.

Bibliography

Birmingham, Stephen, *Our Crowd: The Great Jewish Families of New York*, New York: Harper & Row, 1967.

Chafets, Ze'ev, *Members of the Tribe: On the Road in Jewish America*, New York: Bantam Books, 1988.

Cohen, Steven M., *Content or Continuity? Alternative Bases for Commitment*, New York: American Jewish Committee, 1991.

Evans, Eli, *Judah P. Benjamin: The Jewish Confederate*, New York: The Free Press, 1988.

Fast, Howard, *The Jews: Story of a People*, New York: Dell Books, 1968.

Fried, Albert, *The Rise and Fall of the Jewish Gangster in America*, New York: Holt, Rhinehart and Winston, 1980.

Gabler, Neil, *An Empire of Their Own: How the Jews Invented Hollywood*, New York: Crown Publishers, 1988.

Grose, Peter, *Israel in the Mind of America*, New York: Alfred A. Knopf, 1984.

Hertzberg, Arthur, *The Jews in America: Four Centuries of an Uneasy Encounter*, New York and London: Simon and Schuster, 1989.

Howe, Irving, *The World of Our Fathers*, New York and London: Harcourt Brace Jovanovich, 1976.

Isaacs, Stephen D., *Jews and American Politics*, Garden City, N.Y.: Doubleday, 1974.

Learsi, Rufus, *The Jews in America: A History*, New York: Ktav Publishing House, 1972.

Schwartz, Leo W., ed., *Great Ages and Ideas of the Jewish People*, New York: Random House, 1956.

Silberman, Charles, *A Certain People: American Jews and Their Lives Today*, New York: Summit Books, 1985.

Slater, Leonard, *The Pledge*, New York: Simon and Schuster, 1970.

Wyman, David, *The Abandonment of the Jews: America and the Holocaust, 1941-45*, New York: Pantheon Books, 1984.

RIGHT: GENE WILDER and Zero Mostel in Mel Brooks' Oscar-winning 1968 comedy, The Producers.

A Yiddish New Year's greeting card, c. 1900.

PICTURE CREDITS

AGUDATH ISRAEL OF AMERICA ARCHIVES: 73; AMERICAN JEWISH ARCHIVES: 15 left, 18, 19, 20 left, 21, 22 left and right, 24, 26 right, 27 right, 28 top left, top right and bottom, 29 left and right, 30 left, 31 right and bottom left, 32, 52, 61 left, 67 top left, 71 left and right, 76 right, 77 left, 81, 87 bottom left; AMERICAN JEWISH HISTORICAL SOCIETY: 7 left, 23, 26 left, 30-31 (center), 53, 55 top left, 82 top, 87 top left, 89 bottom; ARCHIVES OF THE AMERICAN JEWISH COMMITTEE: 35; AP/WIDE WORLD PHOTOS: title page, 78, 80; BETTMANN ARCHIVES: 4-5, 6, 7 right, 8, 9, 10 top and bottom, 11, 13 left and right, 14, 15 right, 16, 17, 20 right, 27 left, 34, 36, 37, 38 left, 40 left and right, 42, 43, 44, 45, 46, 47 left and right, 48 left and right, 49 top left, top right, bottom left, bottom right, 50, 54 bottom, 55 right, 56, 60 top left, top right and bottom, 61 right, 64 left, top right and bottom right, 65, 66 left and right, 67 bottom left and right, 68, 69 right, 72, 74, 75, 76 left, 77 top and bottom right, 79 left, 82 bottom, 83 left and right, 84 left and top right, 85 top and bottom right, 86, 87 right, 88, 89 top, 90 inset, 91 left and right, 92 top left, top right and bottom right, 93 top and bottom right; COLOUR LIBRARY BOOKS: 12; HERSCHEL BENDER, ARTET COLLECTION: 25, 63 right; LEORA KAHN: 57 left and right; LESLIE-BART: 85 left; LESTER GLASSNER COLLECTION/NEAL PETERS: 63 left, 84 bottom right, 92 bottom left, 95; MEREDITH GREENFIELD: 59; MONTANA HISTORICAL SOCIETY, HELENA: 25, 39, 41 bottom left; KENNETH S. SIEGEL: 79 right, 90 bottom; SPECIAL COLLECTIONS DIVISION, UNIVERSITY OF WASHINGTON LIBRARIES: 33 and endpapers; YESHIVA UNIVERSITY PUBLIC RELATIONS DEPT.: 41 top

Forward quote in caption page 43 taken from *While Messiah Tarried*, by Norma Levin, New York: Schocken Books, 1977. Quote in caption on page 44 taken from *How the Other Half Lives*, by Jacob Riis, New York: Charles Scribner's Sons, 1890.

PACIFIC
YELLOWSTONE PARK LINE
RTHERN PACIFIC
TICKET OFFICE.
WAY & STEAMSHIP TICKETS
STATES, CANADA & EUROPE